Living in an Icon

Facilitator Guide

A Program for Growing Closer
to Creation and to God

Jerry Cappel &
Robert Gottfried

CHURCH
PUBLISHING
INCORPORATED

Church Publishing
19 East 34th Street
New York, NY 10016
www.churchpublishing.org

Cover design: Jennifer Kopec, 2 Pug Design
Interior layout: Beth Oberholtzer Design

A record of this book is available from the Library of Congress.
ISBN-13: (9781640652385) (pbk.)
ISBN-13: (9781640652392) (ebook)

Contents

Introduction

"The external deserts in the world are growing, because the internal deserts have become so vast." —Benedict XVI[1]

Living in an Icon: A Program for Growing Closer to Creation and to God addresses the deep problem identified by Pope Benedict by providing a structured program of spiritual development that not only helps participants grow closer to God but explicitly involves nature in the process.

Living in an Icon has grown out of years of experience working with the Opening the Book of Nature program.[2] Opening the Book of Nature typically occurs as a single experience over a weekend or several days. However, our experience shows that while participants find such a weekend experience valuable and potentially life-changing, they often desire a longer involvement with group support to more fully incorporate their experience into their lives once they go back home. *Living in an Icon* is our response to that need.

The Spirit moves strongly when individuals pray together. As Jesus said, "Where two or three are gathered in my name, I am there" (Matt. 18:20). The mutual support that comes from sharing these experiences as a group also deepens learning and provides motivation to keep going. It's all too easy to let the pressures and distractions of life intrude when one attempts to do this alone. Going through these exercises with other like-minded people creates a community of practice, something many find lacking

---

1. Benedict XVI, *Homily for the Solemn Inauguration of the Petrine Ministry* (April 24, 2005), AAS 97 (2005): 710.

2. See http://nrccc.org/site/Topics/Resources/BookNature/Book-of-Nature_Main.html.

in their church experience. As such, this program can serve as a key component of a church renewal program.

This is challenging work requiring sustained practice, and participants will need both guidance from a leader and support from their fellow pilgrims. While individuals can do this program on their own, they will benefit far more if practiced as part of a group. This facilitator's guide will provide the background, concepts, and practices you will need to lead a small group of pilgrims on this journey.

A Wider Communion

Living in an Icon draws heavily on Roman Catholic and Eastern Orthodox spiritual practices as a sure grounding for these journeys. However, people from a wide variety of Christian and other faith traditions find them applicable to their own faith experience. While the practices in this program are intentionally couched in a Christian context, they are adaptable to people of wide religious experience and are helpful to participants from other faith traditions (or none at all). Therefore, the program should not be seen as appropriate for practicing Christians only. The basics of gratitude, listening, noticing, and recognizing the divine as present in all things are principles basic to all religious traditions (and common to all human experience). Nature's beauty and interconnectedness is a common experience across all human experience, and *Living in an Icon* can serve as a program that unites people in a common journey of seeking God in deeper ways. These practices bring us together and foster love and respect for the whole diversity of creation, including human diversity.

Reflect on Community: Think back to points in your life when you experienced significant transformation or change in your personal journey. Who was there with you? What role did they play? How might a similar dynamic be important to the journey of a group gathered for *Living in an Icon*?

Learning from the Monastic Tradition

Classic monastic spirituality generally stresses two components of growth on the path to communion with God and the direct experience of God beyond words, thoughts, or images.[3] One component is *asceticism*, which is the work of removing habits and approaches to life that hinder our relationship with God. These include attitudes such as impatience, resentment, anxiety, and self-centeredness. This work resembles cleaning the window of the soul so God's light might shine through it more fully. This window-cleaning process makes space for the development of new dispositions such as patience, gratefulness, and other-centeredness that mirror the qualities of God.

The second component is *natural contemplation.* This involves learning to encounter God in the works of God's hands and the experiences of life. Just as an artist reveals something about herself in her paintings or sculpture or a musician in his compositions, so does God reveal Godself in rivers, oaks, chipmunks, and people. The work of natural contemplation cultivates our ability to hear and see God in everything around and within us.

Think of your eyes as windows to the soul. Asceticism removes the dirt (or cataracts) that keeps light from entering our eyes. Natural contemplation sharpens our perception of what we see. Between them, they open the eyes of our soul to see the everyday world in a new way, training us to see below the surface of all creation and encounter the God who calls out to us from within all of life. *Living in an Icon* blends both asceticism and natural contemplation, engaging in both processes simultaneously.

> **Reflect on Asceticism:** In what ways have you experienced the freedom to seek God with all your heart, mind, soul, and strength? What habits of mind and heart have held you back? What does it take to truly change?

---

3. For a more in-depth understanding of asceticism and natural contemplation, see appendix two.

At the heart of these practices is the old advice for railroad crossings: "Stop, Look, and Listen." Stopping, looking, and listening helps us to develop our spiritual senses and go deeper than what our eyes and ears (and nose, tongue, and skin) normally tell us, so that we may perceive the spiritual dimensions of those things. But we first need to slow down, stop what we're doing (outwardly and inwardly), and notice the things around us. Then we need to learn how to see and hear spiritually. This program selects certain practices and principles from monastic spirituality and combines them in a sequence to facilitate the participant's growth in this spiritual listening.

However, the wisdom of the railroad crossing insists upon one more thing. When we stop at the crossing, we must respond to what we encounter there. We either wait patiently for the train to pass or proceed to cross. To fail to respond appropriately has consequences. Similarly, once we have developed our spiritual listening, we then need to develop our capacity to respond appropriately to what we have experienced. Thus, we might summarize our approach as "Stop, Look, Listen, and Respond."

All of Life Is an Icon

Because all life comes from God, *Living in an Icon* does not create separations between the natural and the human or the body and spirit. The practices of *Living in an Icon* stress the oneness of all experience as an approach to life. It recognizes that God reveals Godself in all things and that the movement of God's Spirit can be found wherever we are and in whatever we are doing. In other words, even though natural creation plays an integral role as a setting for practice and learning, love for nature is not the goal. The goal is contemplation and prayer within all of life, both natural and human. The program strives to develop an approach to life that makes all of life a prayer, helping people to "pray always." By growing spiritually in a manner that includes all creation, human and nonhuman, we heal the false divisions we have created between us and the rest of creation. This healing brings about a reconciliation with God and the community of God's creation so that, ultimately, all things might be drawn to Jesus and "God may be all in all" (1 Cor. 15: 28). This is the good news of the gospel, the goal of God's redemptive work in Christ.

Because many people experience God more easily in natural outdoor settings away from the distractions and emotions associated with human-built environments, *Living in an Icon* applies lessons first learned outdoors to life indoors and within. God's hand in nature, when we take the time to stop, listen, and pray in that setting, can in turn teach us to apply what we learn to life in human society. In many ways, nonhuman creation serves as our monastery where we first learn how to pray and relate to one another.

> **Reflect on Places and Spaces:** Take a moment to think of two places you know: 1) a very "human-built" place, full of human activity, and 2) a very "natural" place, untouched by human activity. What feelings do you associate with each? How might each place influence your inner composure, openness to others, and awareness of God?

This structure of moving from the natural to the human-built is important for many people because of the anxiety, despair, or restlessness we commonly associate with our human-built environments. It is easier for most people to slow down, listen, and reflect in the slowness and quiet of natural places. The challenge then becomes doing the same in our busy everyday lives.

Key Concepts Used in This Program

Several key concepts drawn from monastic practice are used throughout this program. For a discussion of *ora et labora*, see the Taking It Home section of Chapter 13, "Giving in Love." You can find information on *lectio divina* in the *Living in an Icon* participants' book on page 110. For more background on the concept of Beauty, see the first Beauty session in the participants' book and the second appendix in this volume, "A Primer on Asceticism and Natural Contemplation."

The sections that follow provide some background and information you will need to lead a group in this learning process: 1) a summary of the exercises and how they relate to one another, and 2) some practical things to consider when running this program. The appendix contains a more in-depth, scholarly examination of asceticism and natural contemplation for those who desire more background on the roots of this program.

The Exercises of
Living in an Icon

This course is aimed at developing the participant's ability to stop, look, listen, and discern the promptings of the Holy Spirit in the world around, within, and between. Engaging the exercises of *Living in an Icon* builds participants step-by-step toward perceiving God in all things, breaking down the barriers of unawareness and indifference (whether human or nonhuman), and developing their ability to give themselves lovingly to all. In combining the practices of both asceticism and natural contemplation, this is accomplished.

The sessions proceed in an intentional way, each building upon the other and expanding the experience. This order of things matters, and we strongly encourage you to proceed through them in order unless you have a compelling reason to do otherwise.

While there are twenty exercises in total, they can be gathered into three groups, each comprising a sort of journey with a destination. While each journey can be taken as an independent experience, they are meant to be taken in sequence, one building upon the other.

Journey One: Waking Up (Exercises 1-6)

In this initial path to wonder and surprise, participants begin with the fundamental work of stopping, looking, and listening. As they progress through journey one, they are led to increasing awareness and appreciation of what is around them and within. They are prompted to not only observe and attune, but are invited into a response of gratitude and thanksgiving. Gratitude and thanksgiving are the most fundamental of spiritual attitudes and the very foundation of true relationship.

Journey Two: The Road to Kinship (Exercises 7-12)

In this next path, the participants are led to deepen their engagement with what they encounter in their practice. This deepening of experience involves the challenging work of hospitality, humility, and openness to suffering and death. But these dimensions of life are essential to deep abiding and authentic relationship. A true communion with all of creation in the face of the fullness of life and the reality of death is the destination of these practices.

Journey Three: Encountering the Burning Bush (Exercises 13-20)

In this final path to faith and hope, the participants are led to an awakening to the presence of God as Beauty and God's work of love and redemption. Participants are invited to consider their role as conduits of God's love and beauty, and how they might practice the presence of God in the world.

What follows is a brief description of each practice, in the order they were designed to be followed. To prepare yourself to lead others in these exercises, we encourage you to consider how each exercise is a step within a widening circle of stopping, looking, listening, and responding. As you read about each exercise, notice how each builds upon the previous ones, leading the whole group of participants together in a common journey.

Journey One: Waking Up

Exercise One: Reorientation

The first exercise, reorientation, reminds us that as we engage in the exercises in this program, we need to center on our commitment and purpose. The entire series of exercises forms a singular practice of reorientation. We turn away from those things that would distract us from our intention and turn toward those things that attune us to God. The church classically calls this process of turning and returning "repentance." Repentance, when understood more as a renewed intention than as a response to guilt, actually motivates and frames all of this journey. Properly understood, it means turning to the source of light that dispels the dark things in our lives. It emphasizes a positive "turning to" rather than a negative "turning from."

The dual practices of asceticism and natural contemplation nicely fit these twin movements of "turning from" and "turning to." Disciplines of asceticism are practices of turning from while disciplines of natural contemplation are practices of turning to. Taken together, with gladness and hope we turn away from that which keeps us disconnected from God and turn toward that which connects us to God. The key to opening the door to the spiritual life begins with *noticing*. We can't respond to the Holy Spirit if we are not aware that it tugs at our shirtsleeve. Noticing requires attention. Attention requires focus. Focus requires steady attunement. Steady attunement takes practice.

Facilitator's Note: For many, the word "repentance" carries negative connotations that may impede them. So these sessions instead use the idea of "reorientation." Reorienting includes the dual commitments of asceticism and contemplation—listening and responding. We reorient our lives so that we might listen and respond. Hearing God speak to us requires that we be awake and aware of the world around and within us

In addition, we cannot embrace the love to which God calls us if we remain in emotional isolation and mental distraction. God calls us to *be* love, to love God and all of God's works. We can't love God's works if we are unaware of them. Nor can the work of God's hands lead us to the fullness of God if we are not open to them. Natural contemplation involves the work of connecting to that which is around us and openly accepting it as it is without adding our own layers of assumptions, likes, dislikes, and judgment upon it. As we have said, this is the beginning of love.

Exercise Two: Noticing

Once we commit to the whole journey of reorientation, the next step is to stop and notice. Noticing requires us to slow down and to take time. It asks us to be aware of the large and the small around us, and step toward developing "eyes that see and ears that hear." Noticing involves acknowledging that something is already present before us that is worthy of our attention and significant in its own right. All too often we go through life unaware of the other beings in our surroundings as we are caught up in a world of noise, hurry, and distraction. This is the heart of the practice of noticing: experience what is there without judgment, preconceived ideas, or valuations. This is the practice of getting our own noise out of our way that we might hear God speak to us through the Book of Nature.

Facilitator's Note: In this practice we encounter the first note in the participant materials. These brief asides will either amplify an aspect of the practice or draw attention to something that will enrich and facilitate our practice. Be sure to bring them to the attention of your participants. The note on embodiment in this exercise calls our attention to the necessity of being aware of our own bodies if we are to grow spiritually.

Exercise Three: Delight, Surprise, and Wonder

This exercise takes the previous session one step further by encouraging participants to be open to the surprising movements of the Spirit. This can be more challenging than one might think. Many of us spend our days following agendas and checking off lists. We thus insulate ourselves from the world around us as we attend to disruptions and interruptions. As we do, we may fail to hear God speaking to us in ways that wake us up and turn us around.

If we only expect God to speak through creation in the ways we expect, we will obviously miss God's speaking to us in the unexpected. God is a God of surprises. Being open to surprise stretches our minds to allow for new possibilities and experiences of God's action in our lives.

Preconceived thoughts limit our perception of God beyond our conception. Surprises can lead us to wonder, which moves us beyond curiosity. In wonder we can experience the amazing and awesome. In wonder we can also experience the common and sublime. Wonder pries open the places in our hearts that may have become jaded by the humdrum routines of everyday life and helps us begin to experience God's presence in everything around us. As such, it lays the foundation for the next crucial exercise.

Facilitator's Note: Encourage your participants to leave their expectations and likes and dislikes behind when they go out. Help them experience this as an adventure, as when children follow a new path through the woods to see where it goes or lift up a rock in a stream to see what might be underneath. Make this a fun, exciting practice.

Exercise Four: Appreciation and Respect

This exercise builds on the previous one by further molding our attitudes toward our fellow creatures. We typically go through our days judging and reacting to things based upon the likes and dislikes already present in our hearts and minds. Sunsets and waterfalls easily elicit our delight. Mud and mosquitoes do not. Nor do difficult people or difficult places. It is very important in this exercise to discourage participants from simply gravitating toward that which they already appreciate and enjoy. It becomes a true exercise when they can begin to appreciate and respect that which they formerly ignored or rejected.

An important aspect of the practice is to notice not simply what is before us, but also our personal reactions to it, especially with things participants find difficult to appreciate. Usually our reactions are based upon how we have previously been affected by something (fear of the unfamiliar, the challenging, the unpleasant). But while the mosquito may be bothersome to us, it is dinner to the bat. While one personality may be difficult to us, it may be a delight to someone else.

This practice of acceptance helps us realize that God delights in everything without exception and that creation has a purpose far beyond our own personal experience of it. So we will find it helpful to cultivate a practice of withholding judgment, accepting things for what they are, and looking for the holiness in everything. Everyone and everything has something worthwhile within itself, even if it is not immediately obvious to us. Thus, we can learn to respect all things as works of God's hands.

Encountering all things with appreciation and respect opens the door to a deeper delight and more generous heart.

> **Facilitator's Note:** These exercises include a Taking It Home practice. These are important because we can't overcome years of habit and "sleep" with a simple hour a week to practice appreciation and noticing, for instance. Devoted monks spend years with every waking moment of their lives developing these habits of mind and heart. We can do the same by cultivating these practices throughout our day. When we gather as a group to recount our experiences each week, we experience a bit of the discipline of daily discipleship to which the monks aspire. So in every session be sure to stress to your participants the importance of "taking it home."

Exercise Five: Concentration: Getting in Touch

We live in a world that increasingly distracts us and makes it difficult to hear and see the presence of God around us. The next exercise, concentration, encourages us to develop the capacity to focus our attention and engage in longer conversations that lead us into a deeper relationship with creation and with God. Our ability to wait with patient silence is challenged from both without and within. Around us are the many distractions of modern life. But within us are the many voices of expectation and judgment. While we can make arrangements to silence the external distractions, it is much more challenging to silence the inner ones. We carry our constant inner dialog with us wherever we go, making commentary on this and that. It too is a noise that competes with the small, still voice of God around us. It challenges our concentration and demands a hearing. Often the content of that inner dialog has nothing to do with the present moment or surroundings. It is full of past, future, and elsewhere. To practice concentration is to practice being in the *here and now*.

Facilitator's Note: The note in this exercise addresses the role of expectations. Our expectations, both positive and negative, can predispose us to either hear creation speak or block our hearing. The more we develop an expectation that God and God's creation will speak to us in some way when we enter into genuine conversation with it, the more likely we are to hear what is said to us.

As we concentrate our attention with patient openness, we increase the likelihood of hearing the still, quiet voice speaking to us. At the same time we need to grow in terms of letting expectations go, including those of meeting God in our practice. This is a difficult edge to walk. Sometimes participants come to depend upon experiencing some "natural high" or "holy encounter" during their practice. They then judge the value of their practice based upon meeting those expectations. This is not true listening and openness. True listening and openness develops the openness to such an encounter while not coming to depend upon it. This is a form of expecting love without demanding it. This is a practice of trusting in God's presence without defining what that presence must feel like. God can speak through the dull and dead as well as through the vibrant and lively.

Learning to detach ourselves from demands of our expectations is a critical part of learning to trust in God. It's a crucial building block in building faith and openness. So be sure to encourage your participants to let go of their preconceived notions, positive or negative, while still encouraging them to trust the Holy Spirit for guidance and support.

Exercise Six: Thanksgiving: The Formation of Right Attitude

Of all the practices, thanksgiving may be one of the most powerful. Gratefulness has a way of reorienting us and of opening us to others (and thereby to God). When we experience delight and wonder in the life we encounter around us, we are led to express our thanks to the One who made and sustains it. This is the beginning of a shift from observer to participant in the wonder of it all. Once we start relating to the world as one big gift and seeing God's presence in all the events of the day, we begin to recognize that presence in the intricacies of our own lives. Gratefulness orients us toward the giver of all good gifts and opens our hearts more and more to God as we perceive God's goodness all about us. By learning to give thanks in all things, we increasingly learn to see things as God sees them, transforming our thoughts and expectations. We begin to withhold our judgments on the value of this and that, and instead begin to trust with grateful patience.

This in turn opens us further to God. Gratitude, as many spiritual masters have said, is perhaps the very heart of prayer. This is because the practice of thanksgiving opens not just our senses of observation and awareness, but it opens our hearts in ways that move us toward that which we see and experience. When we are grateful for something, we are moved to care about it.

Facilitator's Note: Encourage your participants to take seriously the note "On Discernment and Diamonds." At this point some participants may take a mechanical approach to the exercises, thinking that if they're "working on gratitude" they can't work on delight or noticing. Encourage them to learn to discern the promptings of the Spirit and to trust the Spirit to guide them. Together, the practices are developing a toolbox of approaches to our encounters with creation so that for some one tool may be more helpful than another. Encourage your participants to rely on the guidance of the Spirit as to when and how to use the various attitudes and practices they are developing.

Journey Two:
The Road to Kinship

Exercise Seven: Facing Our Mortality:
Letting Go a Bit More[4]

It may seem an abrupt turn to move suddenly from the practice of thanksgiving to that of death, but the practice of facing our mortality invites us to recognize that our life on earth has an expiration date unknown to us. In fact, all that we have been stopping to notice and appreciate has such an expiration date. All the living things surrounding us have roots deeply set in the life and death of that which has gone before.

Through squarely acknowledging our mortality and letting go of illusions of permanence and control, we deepen our thankfulness for the time we do have, the life around us, and the good gifts God sets before us. Developing an acknowledgment of impermanence and mortality also roots our thankfulness more deeply into all of life, and not only that which pleases us. Thus, it represents a "higher octave" of thankfulness, a revisiting of gratitude at a higher level.[5]

---

4. Depending upon the nature of your group, you may feel it appropriate to move this session to immediately after the Love exercises. If your group consists of people who have not had a strong connection in the past to nature, they may need more time to have developed empathy with it. In this case. moving the session to later may make sense. If, however, your group already has a strong connection with nature, then leaving the session here is more appropriate.

5. Thanks to Fred Krueger, the founder of the Opening the Book of Nature program and coauthor of the participants volume of *Living in an Icon*, for introducing us to the idea of "octaves."

Key to true listening and openness is the appreciation of both life and death, love and loss. Our capacity for thanksgiving must be extended to both sides of this coin, lest our practice become shallow and inconsequential. The full spiritual journey learns to both take hold of life and let it go. The full Christian story consists of both Good Friday and Easter. The one cannot be kept without the other.

Facilitator's Note: This exercise marks an important turn in the journey, and you can help your participants by leading them to not rush through this exercise. Some participants may wish to pass over or minimize this topic. Encourage them to share insights about any discomfort, resistance, or sorrow. Invite them to abide without hurry or judgment with any pain this exercise brings to them. Be prepared to respond with kindness and compassion and invite the group to do the same.

Exercise Eight: Reverence

As we recognize the giftedness of life and the giver that bestows life on all things, reverence and respect naturally follows. This exercise, therefore, moves us from an acknowledgment of thankfulness to a deeper acknowledgment of God and our response of worship. It encourages us to see below the surface appearance of things and to attune to the inner presence of God that permeates all of creation. As we stop and listen to the voices of creation, we also seek the Word who writes each of the words we encounter each day. It also leads us to see God in one another, which for some is more challenging than seeing God in nature alone. Help your participants find ways to name the presence of God in that which they experience during this exercise.

Facilitator's Note: A tendency for some participants may be to have a bias for either nature in its "natural" state or people as somehow more "civilized." This may manifest in repeated criticism of human influence or an avoidance of unfamiliar things in nature. In either case, lead your participants to offer reverence and respect for all creation—both the human-built and the natural, the comfortable and the uncomfortable.

Exercise Nine: Hospitality

The exercise of hospitality leads us even more deeply into our own participation in the icon that is life on earth. With the practice of hospitality, we become actors, choosing to make space for others. Hospitality constitutes a higher octave of respect and reverence as it proceeds from attitude and observation to actions. An inner disposition of reverence and respect is incomplete without the outer behavior that is hospitality.

Just as appreciation, gratitude, and respect prepare us to love all we encounter, so does hospitality. Here we are being called to be proactive in creation, not simply receiving and appreciating God's blessing, but extending God's blessing to others.

It is difficult to respect predation, whether it involves the death of an animal or viruses devastating our bodies. Yet learning to welcome all things in life and death and see God beneath all things leads us further into trust and a peaceful openness to all around us. This is a necessary practice, not so we can become peacefully passive about sickness and waste, but so that we can be peacefully empowered to join in the work of healing and wholeness.

Facilitator's Note: It is a challenging concept to grasp how we can be accepting of predation, disease, and disaster while also resisting them. Accepting them does not mean that we believe that God causes "bad" things to happen to us or that they are somehow good things. Rather, it changes our attitudes toward them so that we are better able to join in the work of healing and redemption. Be alert to how the participants struggle with this dimension of hospitality

Exercise Ten: Humility: Turning Outward

The humility exercise necessarily waits for the previous practices because of what it is—the natural outcome of gratitude, wonder, respect, and reverence. This order cannot be reversed. We cannot make ourselves humble any more than we can make ourselves loving. However, now that we recognize more explicitly our tininess before God and our kinship with all creatures, we can attune to the natural result, which is humility. We can recognize that we, like all creatures, are finite and vulnerable, depending upon God for life itself. This helps restore proper relationships within ourselves and the whole community of creation. This true fellowship demands a proper humility, and once recognized, it can be practiced and nurtured.

It may help participants to note that humility incorporates a whole range of feelings, attitudes, and dispositions. While humility is often rightly experienced as a practice of setting limits on one's ego demands, it is also rightly experienced as properly claiming one's right to be present, loved, and respected. Humility is simply the right measure of things—one's power, needs, importance, and role. It is simply a right and proper relationship to others. It is neither self-depreciating nor self-aggrandizing, nor does it participate in the deprecation or aggrandizement of others.

Exercise Eleven: Sharing Creation's Pain

The next exercise, sharing creation's pain, invites us to an important dimension of love—that of being with others' pain. If we remain removed from the pain of those we intend to love, we cannot enter into full communion with them. So at this point in the program, we focus on allowing creation's pain to enter into our lives that we might be fully present to all of creation's experience. If we cannot share its pain, our relationship to creation remains stunted and self-centered. How does the presence of suffering challenge our faith and trust in God's goodness? How can we perceive God's active presence even in the midst of degradation, disease, and violence? How can we remain aware of persistent and pervasive suffering and also see resurrection on the other side? How can we accept both our own culpability in the suffering and our own limits in redeeming it? For if we are to participate in God's healing and redemption of all of creation, we need to learn how to allow God's saving presence and actions to flow through us, for it ultimately is God who redeems the world, not us.

> **Facilitator's Note:** The challenge here is to help participants enter into this dimension of fellowship without becoming diminished by it. Encourage your participants to open not only to the pain around them, but also to their responses within. Are they tempted to despair? Do they compound the suffering of others with their own pain? You may want to lead a conversation around the question, "How can we manage to remain open to pain and suffering without being crushed by it?"

Exercise Twelve: Settling into Silence

The exercise on silence is a practice of deepening the skill of noticing and listening to the Spirit from the previous exercises. This helps us become increasingly present to God and to the world around us. Just as a practice of hospitality opens our eyes to see below the surface appearance of things, so the discipline of silence can attune our ears to the deeper music that moves through all things. It is working on developing what the monks call the spiritual senses when we attune our ears to silence.

> **Facilitator's Note:** Keeping silent for extended periods of time is quite difficult for most people. Thoughts and feelings quickly intrude on their effort and they soon become frustrated and discouraged. Silence, like humility, cannot be grasped. It can only be nurtured. So a key to this practice is to help participants refrain from judging themselves or even resisting the intrusions upon their effort. Advise them that when the noise and distractions come, simply and quietly return to silence each time, with patience and without judgment. True inner silence will come in its own time.

Journey Three: Encountering the Burning Bush

The Love Exercises: Thirteen-Fifteen

We now are moving toward the climax exercises of *Living in an Icon*. Up to now we have been putting into place practices that facilitate opening ourselves to God, each other, and God's creation. The sequence of practices has moved us toward increasing engagement and response to hearing, seeing, and recognizing God in all things. As we stop, look, and listen, we not only recognize the connectedness around us, we are pulled into it with reverence, hospitality, and humility.

We can think of love as the full giving of ourselves to others and the full receiving of them in turn. This involves more than offer and recognition. It is welcome with affection. This fullness is how the three persons of the Trinity relate to one another. The three love exercises invite us to enter into this flow of giving and receiving, to enter into the Trinity's perfect way of relating.

The next three sessions focus on love in three parts. The three practices establish a sequence of growing in that which love calls out from us: giving, responding, and returning. They encourage us to grow into union with God by growing in communion with all our brother and sister creatures. Love becomes the natural response to recognizing the holy fellowship in which we find ourselves. To not move forward into love would be a failure of soul and spirit. Love is the necessary next step.

Exercise Thirteen: Giving in Love

The first love session emphasizes being present to others as fully as possible. This is important, for love is not simply the passive appreciation of a tourist or visitor. It demands our presence. Obviously, this practice alone requires lots of practice. But this is a major key to opening up our relationship with the rest of creation, a key that we have been building toward up to now. For this reason, we have been working on our listening and recognition skills. Now we work on making ourselves fully present to others in response to their presence before us. Now we begin to give ourselves back.

How do we graduate to this next step? How do we practice making the shift from openness and hospitality to the other, and becoming a giver to it? What does it mean to not only acknowledge fellow creatures, but to *receive* them with welcome? In this exercise, invite the participants to ask themselves, "What does it mean for me to recognize these others not only as holy, but also as creatures who draw love out from me?" What is the difference? What does it say not only about the other creatures, but about me and my ability to love?

Exercise Fourteen: Responding in Love

Here love begins to challenge our inner selves as we consider our responsiveness to kindred creation. For it is one thing to feel an affection or appreciation for another. It is quite another to respond to it. Here we begin to engage the question with each encounter: "What is being asked of me and what holds me back?" Here the demand of the fullness of true reciprocal relationship begins to emerge. If we love all creation as kindred, what does that love ask of me?

This session, therefore, represents a higher octave of letting go and abandoning ourselves in trust to God. It offers a challenge to give all we have, including our reticence, to God and become a full participant in God's ongoing creative life.

> **Facilitator's Note:** The note to the second session on love encourages us to expand our capacity to respond to God. As embodied creatures, God calls us to respond not only with our minds and hearts but also with our bodies. Just as David embodied his wholehearted response to God in his dance to God, so we are called to the freedom of responding wholeheartedly with our bodies. If shyness, reticence, or thoughts of embarrassment prevent us from responding fully, then we have an opportunity to let go and more fully enter into the joy of God's freedom.

Exercise Fifteen: Returning God's Love

The last love session goes one step further, asking us to tap into the well of God's love within and around us and to allow God's love, rather than just our own, to return and flow out from us to all we meet. We become not just fellow recipients of the flow of God's love, but channels of it. As we tap into the Source, we become a source. By doing so, we allow God's redeeming love to flow more freely in the world and become more available to those around us. We are challenged to move from recipient to provider when we ask ourselves: What is God giving in this moment? What is my role as a channel of God's love in this place? How can the presence of God's love expand my love?

The challenging movement with this exercise is to discover motivations beyond our own likes, dislikes, and capacities. It is to shift the questions and responses from "me" to "thee." Help your participants listen for and respond to God's will in the moment.

Exercise Sixteen: Beauty

Just as with the love exercises, we have been working toward the Beauty exercise throughout the entire program. But if we introduce this exercise too early, some may limit their openness to beauty by considering only those things pleasing to their eyes and ears. Others may enjoy contemplating Beauty but fail to experience Beauty's call. Perceiving Beauty as more than personal pleasure requires us to hone our ability to recognize God calling out to us from within everything. For this reason, this more advanced exercise comes at this point in the program. Remind your participants that we cannot make burning bushes appear when we want them to do so (nor should we). As with the shy creatures of the forest who are revealed to the one who quietly waits, so it is with Beauty. All we can do is develop ears that hear and eyes that see so that when God does reach out to us, we can hear the voice or see the flames.

> **Facilitator's Note:** The note on healing in this exercise follows up on the skills of discernment we have been developing. We have previously mentioned the work of letting go, trusting, and acceptance, and in this note we focus on the presence of wounds that may impede our ability to stop, look, listen, and love. So as God reveals to us areas where we need healing of hurts, fears, and sadness, we need to turn to God for grace. At this point in the practice, you can only introduce this dimension of healing and wholeness. But while you may be drawn into a participant's particular need for a healing journey, remember that the group exists for a different purpose. Someone needing significant help in this area will require prayer and support in another setting.

Exercise Seventeen: Radiating Beauty

Just as the practice of love moved us toward becoming a conduit for the flow of God's love, so it is with Beauty. This exercise now takes us to another octave of Beauty—that of radiating God's beauty to those we encounter. We tend to think of our spiritual growth in terms of how it affects us. Here, as in the love exercises, we focus on allowing God's presence to move out from us to others. It is part of the process of receiving fully and then passing on God's beautiful presence. We are again challenged to move from observer to provider as we ask ourselves: Where is God's beauty in this moment? What is my role as a channel of God's beauty in this place? How can God's beauty become my beauty here and now?

Exercise Eighteen: Revealing the Children of God

This exercise encourages us to join in the reconciling and healing mission of God. As we engage with joy and hope in the fellowship of God's love, we look outward upon the whole world. As we practice raising our focus beyond our own needs and abilities, we grow into being a source of God's healing and transformation to those around us. We do this by getting out of the way, detaching ourselves from preoccupation with self and seeking to follow the guidance of the Spirit in all we do. This involves a trust and dependence upon God to do the work of redemption in the world. This is key to avoiding the trap of despair and burnout. The purpose of this journey has not been to make us strong for our important work. The purpose has been to make us free to join in God's important work. We've been working toward this goal throughout our practices of building a foundation of faith in God and hope for the world.

Exercise Nineteen: Faith, Vision, and Hope

So we finally focus on trust in God and hope for the world as God sends us out to take our place in the web of creation. Remind your participants that although we have reached the end of the program, this only is the beginning of what is next. We are always at the beginning of the life of God. We always only scratch the surface. Now we continue our practice of what we have learned and deepen our walk with God and our relationship with creation.

You may find it helpful to remind your participants that they have been given a spiritual toolbox of practices from which they can pull out any combination to address the circumstances in which they find themselves. Remind them of the note on discernment and diamonds early on. Encourage them to listen to the Spirit's guidance of how best they can be in relationship with what they encounter. Help them ask: What is needed here in this time and place? Is it recognition? Appreciation? Does this difficult or ugly moment need me to see below the surface for God's presence in it? Does it need forgiveness and reconciliation? Does it need active love and radiant beauty?

Facilitator's Note: A good closing process for the group may be to have each participant share their responses to the following:

1. What has been the most meaningful learning for you in this journey?
2. What do you think will be your greatest challenge in continuing the journey?
3. What word of encouragement would you like to give to the group?

Remind your participants that we never finish these sessions. We constantly need to practice them. They may want to consider starting them over or revisiting certain sessions periodically in order to grow deeper in these aspects of our life with God and creation.

Exercise Twenty: Who Is My Neighbor?

Finally, we love and serve others best when we recognize their true nature as neighbors in creation. These optional activities offer ways of getting more in touch with land and with God. Just as with human relationships, familiarity leads to fondness. Becoming familiar with the songs of the common birds in your area and the names of the trees and plants will help make them family to you. When you drive down the road or walk in the woods, you encounter these neighbors and acknowledge them by name. Similarly, becoming familiar with entire neighborhoods of the natural landscape leads us to deeper relationship with the rest of creation. We each find our place in it.

Finally, becoming familiar with scripture deepens our relationship with God and God's beloved creation. As we learn to read scripture with ecological eyes, pray with ecological ears, and speak with an ecological tongue, we become open to perspectives we may never have seen before. The Bible is rich with God's love for all creation and creation sings with praise in response. Learn to see them, hear them, and join with them.

Running a *Living in an Icon* Program

This section of the manual discusses considerations you, whether an individual or group, will want to take into account when offering a *Living in an Icon* program. These range from how you structure the program to how to serve as a facilitator.

Possible Constituencies

Living in an Icon best serves participants high school age and above. Youth and adult education groups, environmental organizations and creation care groups, spiritual growth committees and prayer groups, church renewal organizations or committees, interdenominational and interfaith groups all may find this program of keen interest. You may want to consider drawing people from various groups as a way of bringing different constituencies together. For instance, many churchgoers are active in environmental organizations but do not see how their faith applies to their activism. By offering the program to these participants, you might bring people from a variety of denominations together, thereby starting to heal divisions between churches and secular environmental groups. Similarly, many churches have separate spiritual growth and creation care committees. Having both groups sponsor *Living in an Icon* brings them together and strengthens their understanding and provides mutual support.

Program Structure

Ideally the program has the following rhythm. *Living in an Icon* has twenty sessions, each of which consists of developing a specific practice. The practices themselves and their sequence are discussed above. Once a week or every two weeks your group would meet at the same location or changing locations that are announced in advance. Each meeting, which might last from one-and-a-half to two hours, would begin with prayer. Then you would discuss the group's experience with the exercise that they have been practicing. They then would go out alone into nature for forty-five to sixty minutes to try a new practice. Upon returning to the group, they then would share their experiences of the new practice, though after awhile the group might decide this no longer was necessary.

If the group takes two weeks per session as opposed to one, participants would agree that they would spend another forty-five to sixty minutes outdoors on their own during this period so that each week they have a period they spend in explicit natural contemplation. Or, of course, some or all participants might prefer doing it together as a group for mutual support.

The Taking It Home part of each session then encourages participants to continue practicing the exercise that they started in nature in the context of their everyday lives. So if the group is focusing on thankfulness, for instance, having practiced being grateful for the creatures they encounter in nature during their group session, they then would practice gratitude for those things or people they encounter walking down the street or down the hall.

Starting with a Retreat

You may consider starting your program with a retreat. One advantage of starting with a retreat is that it provides an initial deep experience and builds community, thereby increasing the probability that your participants will stick to the program over time. It also may provide you more flexibility as you try to schedule your sessions (see the next section). It could begin, for instance, on a Friday night and continue through Sunday morning. Or you could spend a Saturday together from, say, 9:00 a.m. to 4:00 p.m.

Should you choose to begin with a retreat, be sure to pray for the site and the participants in advance (see the section on prayer below). We suggest a program somewhat like this:

Program Activities

1. Introduction: Have everyone share their name and one or two facts about themselves. Review briefly the activities and schedule of the retreat. Offer a prayer asking the Holy Spirit to guide and bless your time together. Tell them that electronic devices distract them from hearing God speak in nature and that they should turn them off. If necessary, they can check them at lunch. Have them consider an electronic fast for the duration of the retreat.

   Refer participants to their book beginning on page 101, entitled "Initial Reflections." This section offers some quotes from the Christian tradition on nature as a book that reveals God's presence to us. Suggest that they glance over the quotes and then share aloud spontaneously any that particularly speak to them. The point of this exercise is to assure them that what they are about to do is firmly within the Christian tradition, and that it is not some New Age activity. If you would like more information on this for yourself, consult the appendix entitled "A Primer on Asceticism and Natural Contemplation."

2. Having divided them into groups prior to the beginning of the retreat, let them know what group they will be in, who their group facilitator will be, and where they will be meeting for their discussions. See the section below on the organizers' role for more information on discussions and how to facilitate them.

3. Go over the discussion covenant with them. Be sure to emphasize that they will be discussing their *experience*, not their interpretation of their experience.

4. Hand out the reorientation chapter for their future reference and summarize it for them. Lead them through the reorientation practice.

5. Then provide the chapter on noticing and have them read it. Answer any questions they might have, then send them out to practice noticing for forty-five to sixty minutes. Remind them that this is a retreat, and that this is a time between them and God. Therefore, they should go out alone in silence. Remember that each facilitator needs to be praying for all the members of his or her discussion group.

6. After the time is up, call them back in and have them go to their discussion groups. Discussion probably will last forty-five minutes to an hour, depending upon the size of the groups.

7. Repeat this process for the next sessions, according to the amount of time you have available. Give them an hour lunch break. People generally lose their ability to concentrate by 4:00 in the afternoon, so either end at this time or give them free time before dinner.

8. End with a thank-you to the participants for their willingness to engage in the exercises. Review how the program will proceed after the retreat and end with a prayer that God will continue to guide each person and speak to them over the coming weeks.

Retreat Structure

The above easily fits into a morning and an afternoon. Should you start the evening before, you could go through step 4 and begin the next morning with the noticing exercise.

It is very important to let the Spirit guide the retreat. Do not worry overly about adhering to the schedule. While order and structure matter, the Spirit matters more. If things advance more rapidly or slowly than you expected, that is fine. Pray and discern how to proceed and leave the rest up to the Lord.

Should the retreat extend through Saturday night, we have found it particularly important to share the evening meal together and then, if possible, to have a sing-along. Invite people to bring instruments and to join in by singing and playing. Campfires are wonderful for this, but a fireplace or candles in the center of the room can work also. Music has a way of opening our hearts to one another and to God. It builds community in a magical way. If the retreat extends to the next morning, then you may want to do the next session in the series, asking people to bring something back with them that spoke to them. If you wish to end with a worship service, you could choose some scripture passages that speak to the experiences your participants have had during the retreat and/or ask them to bring some passages themselves. Sing some hymns that all know or bring some hymnbooks. If possible, choose hymns that refer to nature and God as creator and Lord of all. Ask people to bring their found objects that are meaningful to them and place them on a table as an offering, giving back to God his good gifts to us. You can ask participants to voice their thanks, sharing their prayers out loud or in silence. You can end with participants praying for one another as a sending forth into the remainder of the program. Should the group be affiliated with a liturgical church, you of course can avail yourselves of the appropriate liturgies the church already offers.

If you decide not to end with a service, you can end with people sharing the objects they have brought and why they are meaningful, giving thanks, and then praying for one another as a sending forth. It is important to have some sort of closing to the retreat as well as a sense that this is merely the beginning of a longer process.

Timeframe

Because *Living in an Icon* consists of twenty sessions, each of which may last for one or two weeks, the program easily can take about forty weeks to complete. Inasmuch as the program utilizes outdoor contemplation as its foundation, you may need to consider the time of year when you begin. In many places winter weather poses a serious challenge to nature contemplation. If your winters are cold, you may need to consider starting the program in early spring and ending in the fall. Of course, doing so may run into summer complications if participants tend to take vacations then or find that having children at home complicates their attendance. The Christmas season, however, also poses challenges as most people find that season particularly busy and stressful (ironically!). Should you decide to extend the program past Christmas, you will have to decide whether to try to keep going during this time or to take a break. Either way, you may need to develop a strategy for getting the group reengaged after the holidays because they probably will have had a difficult time engaging the process during this time.

For this reason, we have broken the program into three modules or journeys. This has several advantages over offering one long program. First, some people may find it difficult to commit themselves for nine to twelve months to a program of this nature. Second, these smaller modules can be promoted as basic, intermediate, and advanced units of an overall program. This way participants can have a sense of achievement when they have completed a module, as well as the expectation that they can grow further, should they wish, by taking the next module. Participants can benefit greatly even by taking just the first module, while deepening their connection to God and nonhuman creation by taking the next two. Third, the modules can be offered as Advent or Lenten programs, activities that prepare participants to engage more fully in preparing for Christmas and Easter. Finally, this format gives you more flexibility in their timing and scheduling. Starting with a retreat that covers the first few sessions also can add to your flexibility.

These considerations may dictate whether or not you tend to spend a week or two weeks on each practice. While two weeks per session provides more opportunity to let that session sink in and become more firmly established compared to allowing one week per session, you may find that you need to compromise given weather and other considerations. You might consider getting feedback from participants as they engage in each session and discern whether they need to extend a session you had intended to practice for one week into a two-week session, or whether after one week they feel they have sufficiently incorporated a practice so that they can proceed to the next. Utilizing a mix of one- and two-week sessions may help you overcome timing issues.

Location

When you are deciding where to hold your weekly or biweekly meetings, look for a site that offers as much of a natural setting as possible given your location. This could be a state park or even a garden. What matters most of all is the availability of solitude, of being away from lots of people, distractions, and interruptions. Because the sessions are times of prayer, your site must offer privacy and the opportunity to be alone with God. This also implies that it be large enough to afford each person in your group a place away from others in the group.

Be sure that your choice of locale is accessible to those who would come. If you anticipate people who are in wheelchairs or who have difficulty negotiating rough terrain, be sure that they can take advantage of at least some places in your site.

Similarly, your site ideally should offer a variety of topographical and botanical features such as streams, overlooks, boulders, fields, woods, and glades. Different types of settings tend to offer different spiritual experiences, so look for a place that offers a variety of opportunities or periodically change your locale so that over the weeks your participants encounter a variety of settings. The more natural the setting, the more easily people will be able to engage in these sessions. However, nature exists all around us, even if it is only a potted plant. So don't be discouraged by urban settings. Seek, as best you can, a locale that offers quiet and at least a modicum of natural beauty.

Finally, be sure that something like a picnic shelter, tarp, or porch is available in case of heavy rain. Slightly adverse circumstances, such as rain or cold, can provide rich opportunities for contemplation. Truly difficult circumstances, however, challenge contemplation for the majority of people. Sharing one another's experiences does require a place where people can discuss in reasonable comfort without the distraction of water running down one's neck or into one's shoes. So choose your locale accordingly.

Note that if weather is too awful to be outside, you can bring nature inside to a degree by having a place you can go that has large windows, or by bringing flowers, leaves, shells, rocks, or nature photos to an appropriate building and having participants encounter the things you have brought.

Taking It Home

It's all too easy for many of us to balkanize our lives into times of prayer and then everything else. We may talk with and seek God, for example, first thing in the morning and then get on with what we think of as our life. Our goal here is to incorporate those practices that we learn in our biweekly outdoor sessions so that we have only *one* life, a life characterized and enveloped by an openness to, and seeking for, God. In this approach to life, no difference exists between secular and sacred. Everything we do flows from our desire to come closer to, and mirror more fully, the God we love and seek.

For this reason be sure to stress the Taking It Home portion of each session, as well as the practices of daily prayer, journaling, reflection, and scripture study that the introduction to *Living in an Icon* encourages participants to begin or to continue. In a world where we all too often relegate our religious life to Sunday mornings, we need to present an alternative understanding that our spiritual life provides the matrix or context for all that we do. Impress on your participants that while what we are asking of them is enjoyable and fulfilling, it also is challenging and the beginning a lifelong journey.

Organizers' Role

Your role includes three basic elements. The first, of course, involves providing the organization and logistics so that all runs smoothly. This includes the clear and timely communication of meeting places and times as well as the making of any necessary reservations.

The second element is perhaps the most crucial—praying for your participants. Your most important role is to invoke God's presence and guidance throughout the program.

The third element of your role as organizer consists of facilitating discussion. Remember that you are a facilitator, not a teacher, guide, or counselor. You do not need to be any more adept at contemplation than anyone else in the group to serve in this role. Neither must you have studied any more than anyone else. What you do need to do is to help the group learn from one another.

The following subsections consider each of these aspects of your service.

Establishing Discussion Groups

Whether leading the discussion at the beginning of each biweekly session or the one after participants have come back from their contemplation outdoors, consider the size of the group. Groups anywhere between roughly five to twelve persons in size are ideal for discussion. If they are too small, there may not be enough variety in experiences to lead to much learning. If they are too large, not everyone may have the chance to share or to share fully. You may need to divide your participants into several discussion groups, each with a facilitator, if your group is large. If you have several groups, consider whether you should change their composition periodically or keep them constant. Changing them gives participants the opportunity to learn from a broader group of people, while keeping their membership constant provides the opportunity for developing deeper relationships with one another. This is a matter for your discernment.

Prayer

Begin and end each session with a prayer. It could be a psalm, a prepared prayer, or a spontaneous prayer. You may choose to offer the prayer at the beginning of the program. However, as the group gels, you probably will want to ask others to lead the prayer or to volunteer to do so.

Before the group assembles, pray for all of them that the Holy Spirit will guide and protect them and prepare them for their time together. Pray for them during the week. Before the group assembles for their next meeting, pray for the site that God would fill it with the light of the Holy Spirit and drive out any influences that might hinder the group's receptivity to the actions of the Spirit. Then, at the biweekly session as the group goes out to contemplate, and during the middle of that time, pray for each of them by name. Finally, pray while you lead the discussions, or while you participate in them if you yourself are not facilitating. As a servant of your participants, shepherd them along the road by interceding for them. *Bathe your participants in prayer during and between the group sessions.* This may be the most single important thing you can do to ensure the success of the program.

Finally, pray for your participants each day between sessions. Remember that the Holy Spirit is the teacher and motivator, so that your most important role is to ask the Spirit to bless and guide each of your participants during each day of the program.

Leading Discussions

In the discussions we focus on our experiences, not on our interpretations of the experiences. Our focus is on how God has touched each person. Thus, we share what actually happened and the effect that that experience had on that participant. On the other hand, we avoid any discussions of theology that we might use to explain the experience, as well as political discussions of any kind or discussions about social, religious, or church issues. These are times to share our personal experiences of our time with God in God's creation, not times to reflect on what these might mean theologically, politically, or socially. Consequently, it is very important to establish the following ground rules for discussions and have all agree to them.

Discussion Covenant[6]

1. Be who you are. Be honest with yourself and one another. Here we can leave titles, achievements, and roles behind. Focus on God and allow the other participants to do so. Honor your common seeking.

2. Stay focused on *what* you and others experience. Many fascinating things may come up during the course of the discussion. However, our goal here is to learn from one another by sharing what happened when we went out to contemplate. Speculating about what might explain an experience or discussing environmental issues that the experiences bring up, for instance, diverts us from listening to one another and gets us back into ideas. Here we are delving into our hearts, not our minds. Similarly, we will not discuss theology or attempt to interpret the meaning of ours or others' experiences. Our focus is on what happened, not on how we understand that experience.

3. Avoid criticism of participants' perceptions about their own experiences. In our discussions we strive to learn from one another's encounters with creation. We all have our cultures and preconceptions that color our experiences, so if someone says something about their experience with which you disagree, say nothing. Our goal here is not to prove we are right or to win an argument. If someone says they experienced something in a certain way, that's the way they experienced it. Honor their experience and their understanding of it. Be generous and charitable. Attempts to correct one another can divide us, whereas love and respect draw us together. Our discussions provide the opportunity for us to learn what it means to live in community.

4. Respect one another's beliefs. Similarly, respect one another's beliefs. Respect does not require our agreement with what others say. It does involve acknowledging that the person

---

6. This covenant is based on the "Rules of Engagement" in the Opening of the Book of Nature program.

with whom we disagree is God's infinitely valued creation in whom we can discern God's presence.

Should you wish to pass out this covenant to your participants, you will find a copy in the appendix that you can use to print out.

Discussion of the Previous One or Two Weeks

After opening with prayer, ask participants how they have fared in practicing the last session, in "taking it home." What challenges did they face? What "successes" did they experience? What did they learn in the process? The goal here is to encourage one another in their daily practice and to help one another learn from each other's experience.

Discussion of Their Experience during the Session

After participants have returned from their forty- to sixty-minute contemplation, welcome everyone calmly and ask who would like to share what happened when they went out. People often are reticent to be the first one to share. Be patient and wait for someone to volunteer and someone will. Don't be afraid of silence. Encourage people to share what they did, what they experienced, and how they felt. If someone says, for instance, "I saw ants going up and down the tree," say something like "Very good. How did you feel when you noticed that?" Or if someone shares that they were attracted by a beautiful flower, encourage them to share how it is that they came to notice the flower. When they saw the flower, what did they do? What did they feel? How did they respond to seeing the flower? By asking questions such as these, we can glean attitudes and approaches to nature from which we can learn.

As people share, take notes on what they said. You might have one person taking notes and another person leading the discussion. If not, the facilitator leads the discussion and takes notes while doing so. The notetaker may find it helpful to underline the verbs the person uses to share their experience because verbs provide clues to the actions they took that led to their experience. Highlight or note how the person felt, because this provides information to the group on the spiritual effect this practice had on the person. You also may find some theme underlies different participants' sharing, such as joy, peacefulness, or awareness of their mortality. Note the theme. You will use these notes to summarize the experience of the group at the end of the session.

Part of your responsibility as facilitator lies in keeping the discussion focused on respectful, loving listening to one another. Sharing our personal experiences with one another builds community and facilitates the movement of the Holy Spirit. Discussion of potentially controversial topics easily leads to division and negativity, which impede the flow of the Spirit.

Should someone start to veer away from personal sharing, gently remind them that we are sharing our experiences, not ideas, and lead the discussion back to where it needs to go. If someone continues to disrupt the discussion, as soon as you can do so in a nondisruptive manner, take them aside and gently ask them to remember the purpose of the discussion and to ask their cooperation in helping the group proceed. Often those who would be argumentative just need to be reminded that experiences are neither right or wrong, they just are. We all can agree that Jean says she experienced what she experienced. We don't have to believe in the experience ourselves or to judge it. What we do need to learn is how to honor one another and to give each other the freedom to share. Remind them that this type of discussion helps us learn to love one another and to get to a place where we place people above ideas and preconceived notions.

In all your relationships with the group *be relentlessly positive.* If someone shares something you think is really trivial or silly, smile and thank them for sharing. This encourages them and provides a safe environment for everyone to share. *Avoid all negativity.*

When one person has shared, ask who wants to go next. We generally have found that it's best to let people share when they feel ready to do so, rather than, say, going around in a circle and having everyone share in turn. This way people feel freer. If someone really doesn't want to share, that's fine, though rare. Give people time.

At the end of the discussion, the facilitator, or the notetaker if there is one, reviews her or his notes and looks for lessons that the Holy Spirit has taught during the session. What did people do that enhanced their experience of the practice? What themes seemed to emerge? What does the Spirit seem to be saying to us?

Running the Program at a Distance

It is possible to run this program at a distance, though it benefits greatly by a least beginning with a retreat of at least a day where participants begin the process as a group. As we said earlier, the Spirit tends to move more strongly when people pray together rather than by themselves. Having an initial strong experience encourages participants to continue the program when they don't have the support of the group on a weekly or biweekly basis. We have found that having people buddy up with partners from the group helps. The partners agree to talk, text, and/or e-mail each other periodically to see how they are doing and to share. Of course, some participants will be more dedicated to partnering than others, so this definitely is less preferable than having a group that one sees rather frequently for support. Using conference calls or teleconferencing periodically and/or maintaining a chat group or website-based discussion forum also can help provide support at a distance.

Some Final Considerations

While it may be tempting to change the order of the exercises or to write new ones, we strongly recommend not doing so until you have had a lot of experience in this program. If you do want to experiment and try new things, we encourage you to do so in another setting, perhaps as part of a separate event. The program as it stands reflects a lot of experience that has been incorporated into the sessions themselves, the choice of sessions, and their order. So we do not recommend making changes until you too have had a lot of experience in this program. The authors, however, would welcome any thoughts, comments, or feedback you might have to strengthen it.

Also, in the last session (or earlier) you may want to ask participants where they would like to go once the program has ended. Some may long for some ongoing supportive community that could grow from this group contemplative practice. Others may want to pursue questions such as how best to understand their experiences in light of their tradition's teaching or how to live in a manner that more closely reflects their deeper ties to God's creation. Ask the participants to pray and discern what the Spirit is telling the group and then work together to follow the Spirit's lead.

A Discussion Covenant

Living in an Icon Discussion Covenant

1. Be who you are. Be honest with yourself and one another. Here we can leave titles, achievements, and roles behind. Focus on God and allow the other participants to do so. Honor your common seeking.

2. Stay focused on *what* you and others experience. Many fascinating things may come up during the course of the discussion. However, our goal here is to learn from one another by sharing what happened when we went out to contemplate. Speculating about what might explain an experience or discussing environmental issues that the experience brings up, for instance, diverts us from listening to one another and gets us back into ideas. Here we are delving into our hearts, not our minds. Similarly, we will not discuss theology or attempt to interpret the meaning of ours or others' experiences. Our focus is on what happened, not on how we understand that experience.

3. Avoid criticism of participants' perceptions about their own experiences. In our discussions we strive to learn from one another's encounters with creation. We all have our cultures and preconceptions that color our experiences, so if someone says something about their experience with which you disagree, say nothing. Our goal here is not to prove we are right or to win an argument. If someone says they experienced something in a certain way, that's the way they experienced it. Honor their experience and their understanding of it. Be generous and charitable. Attempts to correct one another can divide us, whereas love and respect draw us together. Our discussions provide the opportunity for us to learn what it means to live in community.

4. Respect one another's beliefs. Similarly, respect one another's beliefs. Respect does not require our agreement with what others say. It does involve acknowledging that the person with whom we disagree is God's infinitely valued creation in whom we can discern God's presence.

A Primer on Asceticism and Natural Contemplation

Stop and Listen: An Approach to Seeing and Hearing God

Getting to know someone well requires the gift of listening deeply and accepting the other for whom they are. It requires "ears that hear and eyes that see." What does this imply? First, a genuine openness to what you see or hear. Engaging in a conversation while lost in thought or distracted by other concerns limits what we can take in and respond to. It is like having a conversation while trying to watch an engaging movie. Neither the conversation nor the movie provides much satisfaction. Truly getting to know someone requires focus and commitment. It requires full attention. But to give your full attention, you must first cease giving attention to the clamoring of competing things. This is stopping.

Second, getting to know someone requires more than listening to words and sounds. It requires the art of reading body language and perceiving the unspoken message of nuance and subtlety. It involves seeing and hearing below the surface appearance of things. This kind of listening requires a full and undistracted presence. This is deep listening.

Getting to know God is no different. Christian holy men and women through the centuries recognized this and developed approaches to life that helped nurture these skills of stopping and listening.[7] In this program, we focus on asceticism and natural contemplation.

Asceticism

Practicing asceticism involves learning how to die to oneself or, put differently, how to discover or recover one's true self. Our habits, appetites, likes, and dislikes are often obstacles to the openness and listening required to hear and follow God more closely. Asceticism is a tool for working with God's work of getting ourselves out of the Spirit's way.

All too often modern Western minds tend to view asceticism as only a process of self-denial for the sake of penance. It is deemed fitting only to spiritual athletes with special vocations of super spiritual life. But when understood properly, asceticism is for everyone because it is the work of releasing those things that stand as obstacles to our truest self. It is something available to anyone with the desire to discover the joy and freedom that comes from welcoming God into our hearts and minds. It also involves developing ways of being that nourish and deepen our relationships with those around us. By growing in such practices as gratitude, humility, patience, and love, we grow in the ability to truly listen and see others for who they really are and not just for who we already think they are.

What Does Asceticism Look Like?

In large part, asceticism is the effort of recognizing and stopping the control that our inner chatter, demands, distractions, attractions, and judgments have on our life choices. Sometimes it involves a form of fasting. Other times it simply requires

---

7. For an excellent introduction to Christian mysticism and spiritual formation, see Thomas Merton, *An Introduction to Christian Mysticism: Initiation in the Monastic Tradition 3*, ed. Patrick F. O'Connell (Kalamazoo, MI: Cistercian Publications, 2008).

abstinence from judgment. Often it requires patience, quiet, and waiting. This process occurs under the guidance of the Holy Spirit. It is less something that one attempts to do and more something with which one cooperates. When we are open to it, the Holy Spirit guides the willing ascetic through daily life, showing her opportunities to exercise patience or love along with the ability to do so. The ascetic learns to attune to the whispers and nudges of the Holy Spirit and to respond to them. The ascetic grows in relationship with God and in the process starts to become more transparent and pliable. Then, as she becomes more patient, loving, and humble, her God, who is patient, loving, and humble, starts to shine forth and manifest Godself to the world through her.

This practice is the struggle to obtain self-restraint and self-control, whereby we no longer carelessly consume everything (and are consumed by everything). Instead, the practitioner manifests the freedom of frugality and abstinence from the clamor of many things. This freedom and self-restraint empowers expressions of love for all of humanity and the entire creation. The ascetic way is "the moving away from what we want as individuals to what the world needs as a whole. It is valuing everything for itself, and not simply for ourselves. It is regaining a sense of wonder and being filled with a sense of goodness."[8]

This gift of freedom and attunement is one of the goals of this program. You, as the facilitator, are encouraged to experience it for yourself either before you engage others in the journey or along with them. This cannot be taught by concept and words alone. It must be experienced and practiced and turned into habit.

---

8. Ecumenical Patriarch Bartholomew, "Faith and Environment: An Inspirational Perspective" (Utrecht, the Netherlands, 2014), 5. See also Pope Francis, *Laudato Si': On Care for Our Common Home* (Vatican City: Vatican Press, 2015), 91–92.

Natural Contemplation

> In order to serve God, one needs access to the enjoyment
> of the beauties of nature, such as the contemplation of
> flower-decorated meadows, majestic mountains, flowing
> rivers. For all these are essential to the spiritual devel-
> opment of even the holiest people. —Moses Maimonides
> (1135–1204)[9]

The biblical writers and holy people throughout the centuries recognized that God speaks strongly through creation, through people and the natural world, so much so that they said that God speaks through two coequal books: the Book of Scripture and the Book of Nature. In both cases God speaks through the "works of his hands," God's creatures, both human and nonhuman.[10]

In the former, God speaks through the authors inspired to write the collection of literature that has come to be known as the Bible. Jesus, the Word of God, manifests himself through the words on the page to those readers who are open to receiving him. Once again, the Holy Spirit opens the eyes and ears of the heart to hear Jesus speak his word to those seeking Him. The practice of *lectio divina,* or sacred reading, attempts to help the ascetic hear the Holy Spirit speak to him through sacred texts. In this practice one reads a passage of scripture slowly, looking for a word or phrase that "pops out" at them. When this happens, the reader then reflects on what the text is saying to them and then allows the word or phrase to move through them, to "rumble around inside" so that over time the words transform the reader into an image of the Word itself.

The biblical writers and saints also recognized that the Holy Spirit blows where it will, speaking to people through all of creation, not just through inspired authors. The early church fathers

9. Moses Maimonides, *Ha-Mispik La-Avodat ha-Shem,* p. 165, quoted in David Stein, *A Garden of Choice Fruit* (Wyncote, PA: Shomrei Adamah, 1991), 66.

10. For example, see Pope Francis, *Laudato Si': On Care for Our Common Home,* 85.

spoke of Jesus as the Word of God. God, through the Word, spoke creation into existence. Moreover, each type of creature, and each individual creature, whether a platypus or a rock, is a *logoi*, or word, of God.[11] *Logoi* goes beyond "word" to connote thought, essence, principle, and meaning.[12] Each creature tells us something about God's thoughts and derives its ultimate meaning from God. Just as Hemingway's books, for example, reveal something about Hemingway himself, so do the works of God's hands reveal to us something about God. Thus, by truly getting to know God's creation, one can come to know a lot about God. Accordingly, Psalm 19:1–4 states:

The heavens are telling the glory of God;
 and the firmament proclaims his handiwork.
Day to day pours forth speech,
 and night to night declares knowledge.
There is no speech, nor are there words;
 their voice is not heard;
yet their voice goes out through all the earth,
 and their words to the end of the world.

St. Irenaeus of Lyons (129–203), for example, further asserts:

For even creation reveals Him who formed it, and
the very work made suggests Him Who made it, and
the world manifests Him Who ordered it.
The Universal Church, moreover, through the whole world,
has received this understanding from the Apostles themselves.[13]

---

11. For example, see Andrew Louth, "Man and Cosmos in St. Maximus the Confessor," in *Toward an Ecology of Transfiguration: Orthodox Christian Perspectives on Environment, Nature, and Creation*, ed. John Chryssavgis and Bruce V. Foltz (New York: Fordham University Press, 2013); Kallistos Ware, "Through Creation to the Creator," in Chryssavgis and Foltz, *Toward an Ecology of Transfiguration*.

12. Pope Francis, *Laudato Si': On Care for Our Common Home*, 51; Louth, "Man and Cosmos," 62–63.

13. Irenaeus, *Against Heresies*, Book II, Chapter 9.1, *Ante-Nicene Christian Library: Translation of the Writings of the Fathers*, ed. Alexander Roberts and James Donaldson (Edinburgh: T and T Clark, 1865), 1:143.

Similarly, Ecumenical Patriarch Bartholomew tells us:

> Nature is a book, opened wide for all to read and to learn. Each plant, each animal, and each micro-organism tells a unique story, unfolds a wonderful mystery, relates an extraordinary harmony and balance, which are interdependent and complementary. The same dialogue of communication and mystery of communion is detected in the galaxies, where the countless stars betray the same mystical beauty and mathematical interconnectedness.[14]

Just as we can sometimes personally encounter God in other people or in the words of scripture, the saints also speak of encountering the Divinity by seeing under the surface of the mere appearances of created things.[15]

St. Paul and St. John both teach that the Word is in all things and that all things are in Him (John 1:10, 14; Col. 1:15–20). St. John of Damascus (675–749) proclaims that the whole earth is a living icon of the face of God. An icon is that which serves as a portal through which one encounters God.[16] Similarly, from the very early days of Judeo-Christianity, its sages have stated that God reveals Godself through Beauty, an experience of the underlying reality within all things.[17] Many commentators point to Moses's encounter with the burning bush as a prime example of God revealing Godself through creation, of

---

14. Bartholomew, "Faith and Environment: An Inspirational Perspective," 5.

15. Francis, *Laudato Si': On Care for Our Common Home*, 80, 88.

16. St. John of Damascus, *Three Treatises on the Divine Images*, Treatise 1:11–16, trans. Andrew Louth (Crestwood, NY: St. Vladimir's Seminary Press, 2003), 26–31.

17. For the ancient Greeks, the experience of Beauty involves the experience of seeing something concrete or tangible while at the same time sensing a seductive otherness. It involves an invitation to the beholder and the beholder's response to it. Thus, Beauty calls out to the beholder. The meaning of the word "beauty" also includes the sense of the orderly arrangement of all the parts of the cosmos. This word captures the sense of divine order, integrity, wholeness, and moral rectitude, as well as of human love of outward appearances. Robert Gottfried, "Beauty by Design," *Sewanee Theological Review* (December 2015): 28–29.

encountering God's transcendent Beauty in an object of everyday life. As Kallistos Ware states so eloquently, "Each created person and thing is a point of encounter with 'the Beyond That is in our midst,' to use Dietrich Bonhoeffer's phrase. We are to see God in everything and everything in God. Wherever we are and whatever we are doing, we can ascend through the creation to the Creator."[18] While creation is not God, God is in all things and all things are in God. Or, as Elizabeth Barrett Browning put it,

> Earth's crammed with heaven,
> and every common bush afire with God;
> but only he who sees, takes off his shoes,
> The rest sit round it and pluck blackberries
> ("Aurora Leigh," Book VII: 821–824)[19]

As we know, it is all too possible to ignore the world about us by passing through it lost in thought or immersed in some distraction from our headphones. Even if the world may be trying to speak to us in any number of ways, we show no interest in listening to it, as we are filled to the brim with the mundane.

Consequently, ascetics must learn not only to practice *lectio divina* with scripture, paying attention to words or phrases that "pop out" to the reader, but also with the Book of Nature; that is, they need to learn to truly see and listen to nonhuman creation, allowing God to speak to them through all of God's creation. Reading the Book of Nature came to be known as natural contemplation or *theoria physike*. While some monastics feel this can be learned only after the adept has grown sufficiently in virtue, others such as Thomas Merton believe that

---

18. Ware, "Through Creation to the Creator," 92.

19. Elizabeth Barrett Browning, "Aurora Leigh," in *The Works of Elizabeth Barrett Browning*, ed. Sandra Donaldson, et al. (London: Pickering and Chatto, 2010), 3:200.

the practices of natural contemplation and ascetic discipline go hand in hand.[20]

Our experience with this program leads us to agree with Merton: the two practices reinforce one another. Nature has much to teach us about patience and humility, for instance. Camping for days on end amidst clouds of mosquitoes can teach us a lot about dealing with the day-to-day annoyances of life and help us develop patience, just as walking in the midst of giant trees and immense mountain valleys provides a wonderful lesson by putting our immense egos into proper perspective and helping us understand more fully that we are not the center of the universe. At the same time, many people state that they feel closest to God in the outdoors, even more than in a church. By becoming open to God in the wild, or in the garden, or the backyard, where encounters with God come most easily, one then can learn to see God in a pot or pan, a pan handler on the street, an icon, or a piece of Shaker furniture. Wherever they occur,

20. Similarly, the third and final stage of spiritual growth may occur along with the first two stages (asceticism and natural contemplation). For instance, When someone reaches insights into creation on the path of his ascetic life, then he is raised up above having prayer set for him within a boundary: for it is superfluous from then onwards for him to put a boundary to prayer by means of (fixed) times or the Hours; his situation has gone beyond its being a case of his praying and giving praise when he (so) wants. From here onwards he finds the senses continuously stilled and the thoughts bound fast with the bonds of wonder; he is continually filled with a vision replete with the praise that takes place without the tongue's movement. Sometimes, again, while prayer remains for its part, the intellect is taken away from it as if into heaven, and tears fall like the fountains of water, involuntarily soaking the whole face. All this time such a person is serene, still, and filled with wonder-filled vision. Very often he will not be allowed even to pray; this in truth is the (state of) cessation above prayer when he remains continually in amazement at God's work of creation—like people who are crazed by wine, (for) this is "the wine which causes a person's heart to rejoice" (Isaac, II: XXV, §1–5, p. 151). Sebastian Brock, *Isaac of Nineveh: "The Second Part"* (Louvain, Belgium: CSCO, 1995), chaps. IV–XLI, quoted in Jonah Paffhausen, "Natural Contemplation in St. Maximus the Confessor and St. Isaac the Syrian," in Chryssavgis and Foltz, *Toward an Ecology of Transfiguration*, 46–58. For an excellent discussions of natural contemplation, see Paffhausen, "Natural Contemplation," 46–58; Ware, "Through Creation to the Creator," 94–95.

these encounters motivate us and help transform us into more God-like, virtuous people.

This interactive process of growth in virtue and natural contemplation returns us to our "natural" state, bringing us closer to the state humans enjoyed in the Garden. A modern writer expresses this well:

> Despite our expulsion from the Garden, paradise still exists. It is all around us, but our entry to it is barred by the Cherub(im) with the flaming sword. The angel with the sword of fire represents not an absolute ring-pass-not, but a spiritual barrier that requires an initiation, a trial by fire, the purgation and transformation of our nature before we are allowed entry, or rather, re-entry. In short, the human soul must heal itself or be cleansed of its disorder if it wishes to participate once again in the paradisal gifts hidden in nature. Our senses must be cleansed of the disfiguring encrustation of selfish passions; our soul must cease its endless agitation in the circle of its self concern; our heart must awaken from its disordered dreams and gather itself together in loving attention. Then and only then is it possible to see again as we are meant to see. This is the spiritual challenge of wilderness; it is a call to stop, pay attention, and see in this way.[21]

In the Garden humans communed with God and all creation, so much so that God entrusted to Adam the task of naming the animals, a task that required an intimate knowledge of the essence of each creature. Adam needed to be able to perceive the *logoi*, or ultimate meaning, of a creature in order to name it because in biblical thought a creature's name captures the essence of that creature or person. Adam was adept at natural contemplation.

---

21. Vincent Rossi, "Glimpses of Paradise: Beauty and the Natural World in the Photography of Christopher Burkett," in *Intimations of Paradise*, ed. Christopher Burkett (Milwaukie, OR: West Wind Arts, 1999), 22.

This process of spiritual growth not only opens us to God's creation but transforms us into more loving, transparent beings through which God's Spirit shines; it removes the bushel baskets covering the light of the Beauty that shines from within us (Luke 11:33). We become more godlike, more who we were meant to be: images of Jesus and the Father. By our individual and corporate growth, then, we make Jesus more manifest in the world. This unleashes in us God's creativity, enabling us to participate in God's ongoing creative activity in the world.[22]

The process of actively engaging with creation under the guidance of the Holy Spirit through work and contemplation leads us to grow in wisdom, an understanding of how things work and how God intends us to work with it.[23] We learn about natural processes and the nature of things and how to cooperate lovingly with them. This involves more than technical or scientific knowledge. It implies an intimate "knowing" of God's creatures, of living in a vibrant ongoing relationship with all around us and of understanding God's will for it.[24] We work and live amidst all beings not just to earn a living and to enjoy responsibly the fruits of creation, but to reveal the hand of God

---

22. Rather than creation being a one-time event, creation is an ongoing process. When the Hebrews spoke of creation, they used the word *beriah*, or "creating," thereby expressing a view of the created order as dynamic and changing. "Creation" is more a gerund than a noun. For more on the dynamic nature of God's creative process, see Terence E. Freitheim, *God and World in the Old Testament: A Relational Theology of Creation* (Nashville, TN: Abingdon Press, 2001); Paolos Mar Gregorios, "New Testament Foundations for Understanding the Creation," in *Tending the Garden: Essays on the Gospel and the Earth*, ed. Wesley Granberg-Michaelson (Grand Rapids, MI: Eerdmans, 1987); Larry L. Rasmussen, "Creation, Church, and Christian Responsibility," in Granberg-Michaelson, *Tending the Garden*.

23. Robert K. Johnston, "Wisdom Literature and Its Contribution to a Biblical Environmental Ethic," in Granberg-Michaelson, *Tending the Garden;* Claus Westermann, *Elements of Old Testament Theology*, trans. Douglas W. Scott (Atlanta: John Knox Press, 1982), 98–100.

24. For an intriguing example of a modern scientist adept at wisdom, see Glenn Clark, *The Man Who Talks with the Flowers: The Life Story of Dr. George Washington Carver* (St. Paul, MN: MacAlester Park, 1976).

through our loving altering of creation. This level of intimacy and knowledge transcends facts (while including them), moving us to maximize meaning and Beauty in the world rather than narrowly defined profit or even broadly construed social (human) benefit.[25]

---

25. For a thorough discussion of these thoughts, see Francis, *Laudato Si': On Care for Our Common Home,* http://w2.vatican.va/content/francesco/en/encyclicals/documents/papa-francesco_20150524_enciclica-laudato-si.html.

Additional Resources

Bouma-Prediger, Steven. *For the Beauty of the Earth: A Christian Vision for Creation Care.* Grand Rapids: Baker Academic, 2001.

Brown, William P. *The Seven Pillars of Creation: The Bible, Science, and the Ecology of Wonder.* New York: Oxford University Press, 2010.

Edwards, Denis. *Ecology at the Heart of Faith: The Change of Heart That Leads to a New Way of Living on Earth.* Maryknoll, NY: Orbis Books, 2006.

Johnson, Elizabeth A. *Ask the Beasts: Darwin and the God of Love.* New York: Bloomsbury, 2014.

———. *Creation and the Cross: The Mercy of God for a Planet in Peril.* Maryknoll, NY: Orbis Books, 2018.

Macy, Joanna, and Molly Young Brown. *Coming Back to Life: Practices to Reconnect Our Lives, Our World.* British Columbia: New Society Publishers, 1998.

Macy, Joanna, and Chris Johnstone. *Active Hope: How to Face the Mess We're In without Going Crazy.* Novato, CA: New World Library, 2012.

Middleton, J. Richard. *A New Heaven and a New Earth: Reclaiming Biblical Eschatology.* Grand Rapids: Baker Academic, 2014.

Taylor, Barbara Brown. *An Altar in the World: A Geography of Faith.* New York: Harper One, 2009.